PADRE ANTONIO SOLER

FANDANGO

Arranged for Two Guitars

BY JOANNE CASTELLANI
AND MICHAEL ANDRIACCIO

Cover Photo by Jim Bush Photography
Cover Art by Michael Andriaccio
Cover Design by Charlie Lee Georgescu

SCORE

Please visit: www.castellaniandriaccio.com

Exclusive Sales Agent: Mel Bay Publications, Inc.
WWW.MELBAY.COM

Editors' Notes

Every effort has been made with this arrangement to remain as faithful to the original composition as possible. However, there are numerous alterations that were deemed necessary in order to facilitate the most effective musical ideas within the confines of the instrument and medium.

This is clearly an arrangement and not a transcription, and music serves as a blueprint for the interpreters' creativity.

The sign, "c. s." Indicates an across the string mordent or trill and is fingered accordingly.

Also Available from Mel Bay:

The Castellani Andriaccio Duo Collection
Concert Masterworks Arranged for Two Guitars
Works by Albéniz, Dowland, Europe-Dabney, Granados, Handel, Matos Rodriguez and Nazareth
https://www.melbay.com/Products/31023/the-castellani-andriaccio-duo-collection.aspx

Joanne Castellani and Michael Andriaccio

The Castellani Andriacio Duo

Joanne Castellani and Michael Andriaccio have enjoyed a celebrated career as one of the foremost guitar duos in the world. They were scholarship students at the master classes of Andres Segovia and studied composition with Aaron Copland, Morton Feldman and Lejaren Hiller. They have received numerous awards and distinctions and have been concerto soloists with the London Symphony Orchestra, the Israel Chamber Orchestra, the Rome Festival Orchestra, the Buffalo Philharmonic Orchestra, and the Chautauqua Symphony among others. Sought after pedagogues as well, they have performed and taught at over one hundred colleges, universities and conservatories around the world.

Recognized as the pre-eminent American Guitar Duo, the nation's capital has embraced them with two National Endowment for the Arts Solo Recitalist Fellowships. They have been featured in concert at the White House, the Smithsonian Institution, and the JFK Center for the Performing Arts. The two have served as Cultural Envoys of the US State Department with tours of Brazil, China and the Philippines. In addition, they are members of the Alice Tully Circle of the Chamber Music Society of Lincoln Center.

Popular broadcast artists on international radio and TV, the duo has been featured on NPR, PBS, BBC and were featured on Radio Nacional of Argentine Public Radio in celebration of Astor Piazzolla's 100th Birthday. Tireless proponents of new music, they have commissioned and premiered numerous works for guitar duo, including two acclaimed concerti by Roberto Sierra, *"Of Discoveries"* and the *"Fantasia Corelliana"*, both works commissioned and given their world premiere performances and recordings by the Duo.

The Duo has recorded ten acclaimed cds, two named "Best of the Year" by Fanfare Magazine and American Record Guide. Critics around the globe from the New York Times to Gramophone Magazine have unanimously praised their, *"elegance, style, poise and exquisite taste in interpretation"*. Currently, Joanne and Michael are the Artistic Directors of the JoAnn Falletta International Guitar Concerto Competition presented by Buffalo Toronto Public Media and the Buffalo Philharmonic Orchestra. Joanne Castellani is Prof. Emerita of the SUNY at Buffalo. Michael's recently released world premier recording of "Goyescana", concerto for Guitar and Orchestra by three-time Grammy and Ace Award-winning composer, Michael Colina, with the London Symphony Orchestra has received unanimous international acclaim. Joanne and Michael are founders of and executive producers for Fleur de Son Classics, Ltd., an internationally distributed independent record label with a catalog of over one hundred and twenty titles, more than half of which are world premiere recordings with Grammy Award winning and Grammy Nominated artists.

Their concert arrangements and transcriptions are published by Mel Bay Publications, Editions Orphee, Oxford University Press, Bill Holab Music, and Subito Music.

Joanne Castellani and Michael Andriaccio use Savarez Strings exclusively.
www.castellaniandriaccio.com

Score

Fandango

Padre Antonio Soler

Arr. Castellani Andriaccio Duo

Fine
Gtr. 1
Gtr. 2
poco rit.
decrescendo
allargando
accel.
a tempo
(Bb)
pont.

Gtr. 1
Gtr. 2
pp
pont.
mf
f

Gtr. 1
Gtr. 2
ff scuro
mf
pont.
allargando
accel.
f a tempo
ff pont.
naturale

Gtr. 1
Gtr. 2
pont.
pizz.
naturale
naturale
c.s. (Bb)
sub.
sub.

99
Gtr. 1
Gtr. 2
(Bb)
sub. p
f
sub. p
mf
102
p
f
p
105
p
p
108
mp
mp
111

114
Gtr. 1
Gtr. 2
f
117
mp
mp
legato
120
f
legato
123
ff
pizz.
legato
naturale
scuro
126
legato

130
Gtr. 1
Gtr. 2
134
Gtr. 1
Gtr. 2
138
Gtr. 1
Gtr. 2
142
Gtr. 1
Gtr. 2
147
Gtr. 1
Gtr. 2
f

Gtr. 1
Gtr. 2
Harms 8va

Harms 8va
Gtr. 1
Gtr. 2
scuro
pont.
naturale
più mosso
poco rit.

PADRE ANTONIO SOLER
FANDANGO

Arranged for Two Guitars

BY JOANNE CASTELLANI
AND MICHAEL ANDRIACCIO

Cover Photo by Jim Bush Photography
Cover Art by Michael Andriaccio
Cover Design by Charlie Lee Georgescu

GUITAR 1

Please visit: www.castellaniandriaccio.com

Exclusive Sales Agent: Mel Bay Publications, Inc.
WWW.MELBAY.COM

Classical Guitar 1

Fandango

Padre Antonio Soler

Arr. Castellani Andriaccio Duo

1/2CII
VII
V
1/2CV
I
ff scuro
pont.
allargando
accel.
II
III
f a tempo

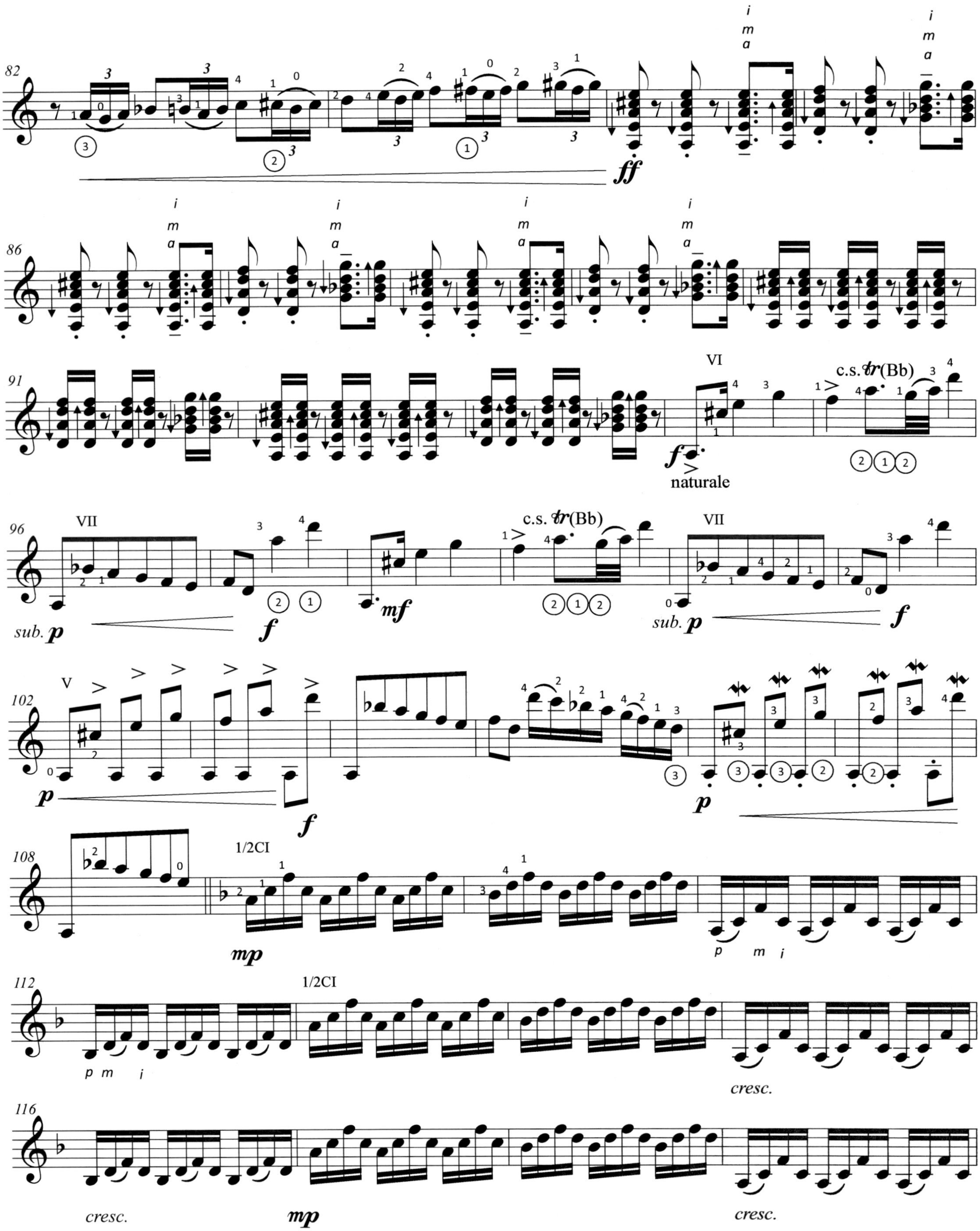
naturale
c.s. tr(Bb)
VI
VII
V
sub. p
1/2CI
cresc.

ff pizz.
legato
naturale
f
ff

* See Editors' Notes

* See Editors' Notes

R.H. fingernails on upper bout
Slap L.H. on soundboard
pont.
naturale

* See Editors' Notes

313
p p i m a
317
1/2CI
mf
323
pp pizz.
329
335
p naturale
p pont.
341
mf
347
mf
V
VIII
1/2CV
p i m
spazioso
351

V
pp pizz.
VII
V
accelerando
f a tempo
naturale

392
398
403
V
VI
VIII
406
D.C. al Fine
Ossia
1/2CV

PADRE ANTONIO SOLER
FANDANGO

Arranged for Two Guitars

BY JOANNE CASTELLANI
AND MICHAEL ANDRIACCIO

Cover Photo by Jim Bush Photography
Cover Art by Michael Andriaccio
Cover Design by Charlie Lee Georgescu

GUITAR 2

Please visit: www.castellaniandriaccio.com

Exclusive Sales Agent: Mel Bay Publications, Inc.
WWW.MELBAY.COM

Classical Guitar 2

Fandango

Padre Antonio Soler

Arr. Castellani Andriaccio Duo

pont.
scuro
allargando
accel.
a tempo
decrescendo
decresc.
crescendo
cresc.
pont.
naturale
crescendo
cresc.
pont.

87
VIII
V
pizz.
naturale
91
VI
III
VI
V
II
III
I
94
1/2CII
mp
sub. p
mp
98
sub. p
mf
102
p
106
p
mp
110
CIII
tr
III
tr
tr
CI
116
III
f
mp
legato
f
legato
122
1/2CII
scuro

legato
V
1/2CV
II
V

168
mp
f
173
mf
f
178
p
mf scuro
(Eb)
p pont.
185
naturale
mf
più mosso
f
1/2CII
191
pont.
poco rit.
naturale
196
a tempo
mp
201
204
II
mf
III
VI
III

mp
f
mf giocoso
p
pizz.

rasqueo
simile
naturale
rasqueo
simile
pont.
tasto

pont.
subito p
naturale
IV
V
III
(Bb)
mp
f rasqueo
simile
CIII
pont.
II
pp naturale

tasto
pont.
spazioso e alla campanella
accelerando
a tempo

legato
D.C. al Fine
Ossia

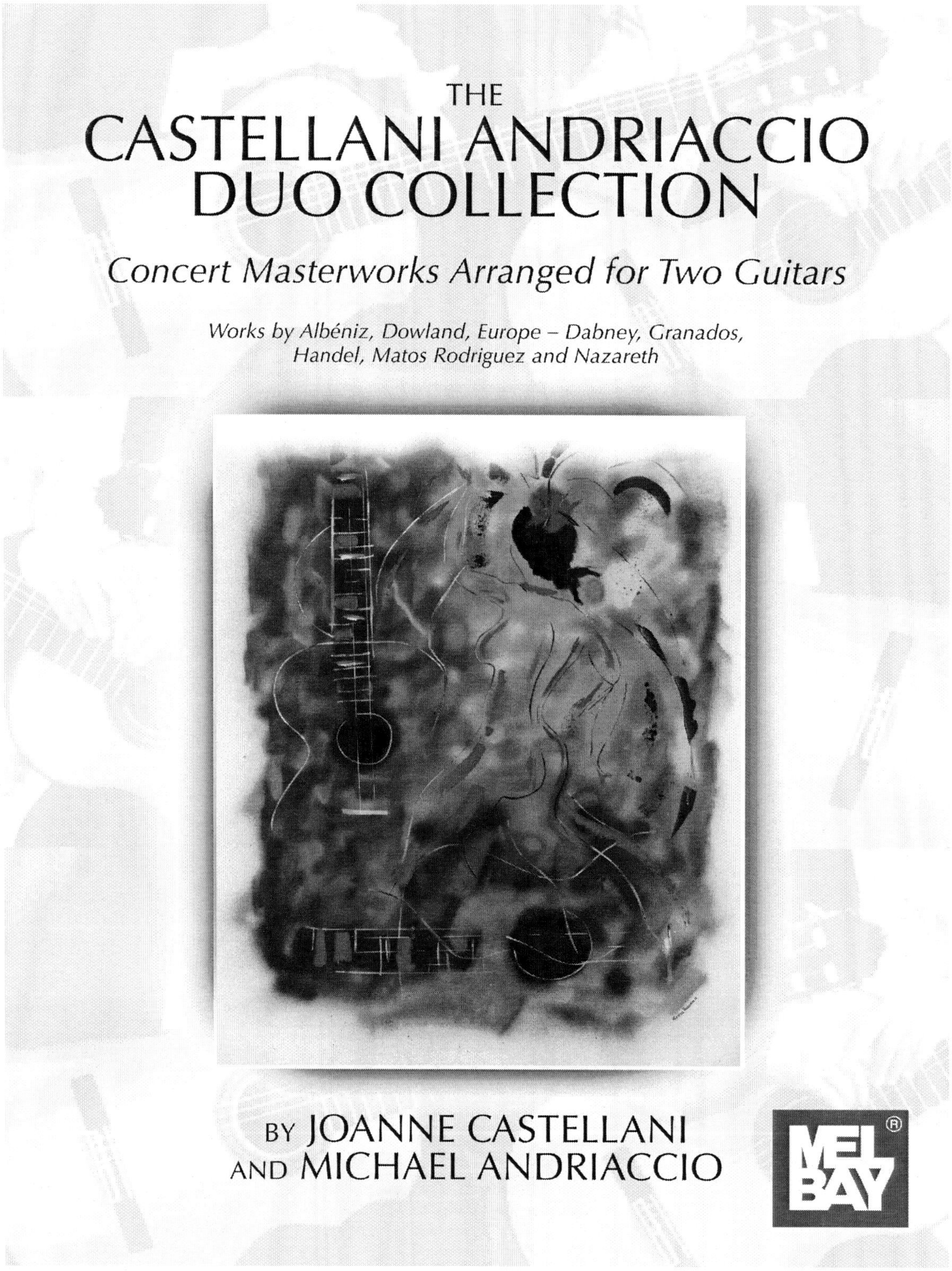

We are pleased to present this collection of masterful concert arrangements that have been a major part of the Castellani Andriaccio Duo's touring and recording repertoire for decades. These arrangements stand out as works of art unto themselves in addition to their place in the broader musical repertoire that they represent. This contribution to the classical guitar repertoire is just one component of the Castellani Andriaccio Duo's legacy to the instrument as one of the foremost guitar duos in history. Includes separate pull-out parts for Guitar 1 and Guitar 2.

* See Editors' Notes

* See Editors' Notes

Gtr. 1
Gtr. 2
238
pp
241
245
249
p
pizz.
252
f
rasqueo
ff
simile
naturale

255
Gtr. 1
Gtr. 2
258
260
262
cresc.
264

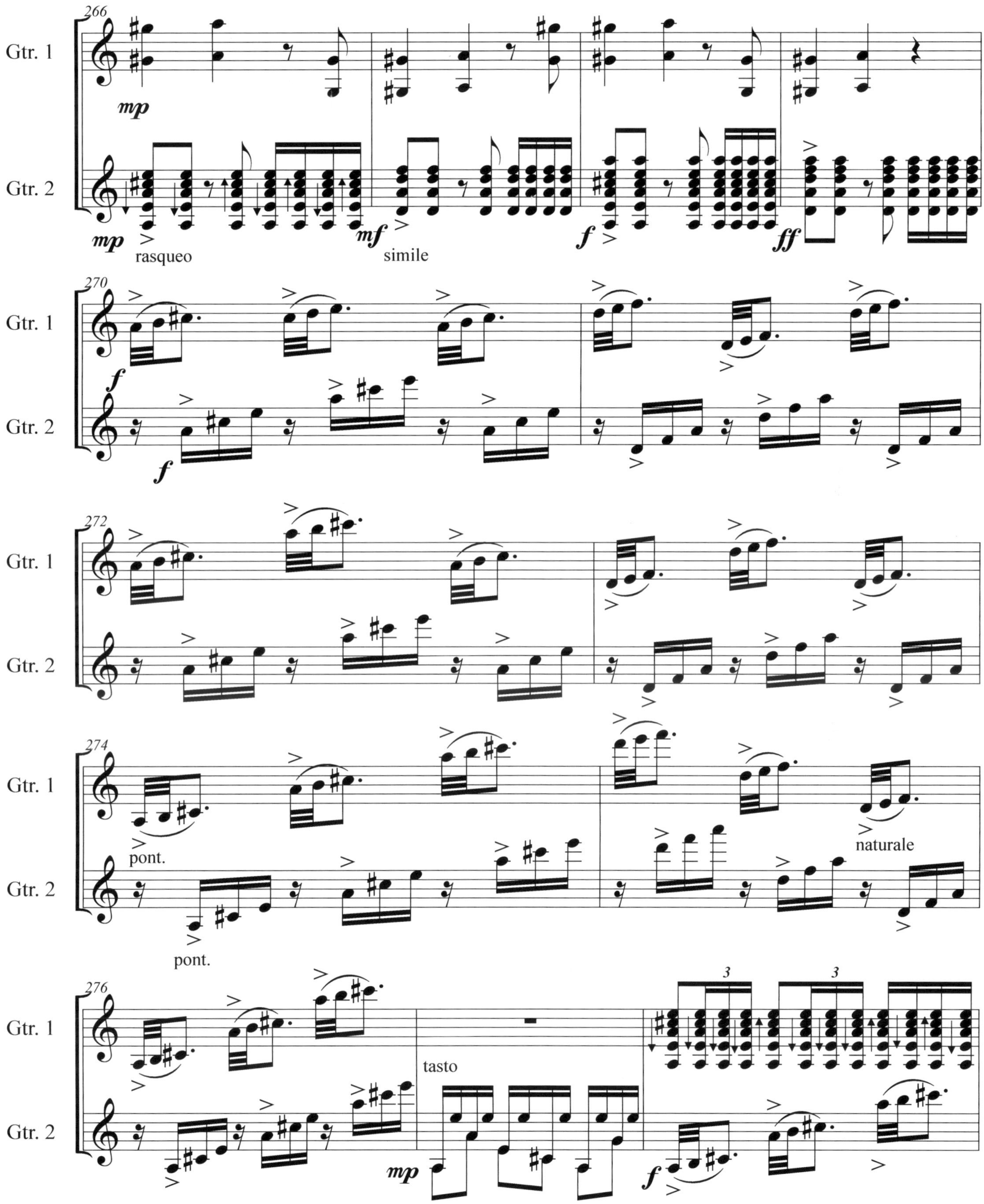
266
Gtr. 1
Gtr. 2
mp
rasqueo
mf
simile
f
ff
270
272
274
pont.
naturale
276
tasto
3

279
Gtr. 1
Gtr. 2
simile
281
pont.
284
subito p
subito p
naturale
289
294
(Bb)

* See Editors' Notes

319
Gtr. 1
Gtr. 2
pp pizz.
pp naturale
324
329
mp
f
mp
334
f
p naturale
mf tasto
339
p pont.
p pont.
f
f

344
Gtr. 1
Gtr. 2
mf
mf
348
spazioso e alla campanella
351
354
357

360
Gtr. 1
Gtr. 2
363
3
367
pizz.
pp
accelerando
372
f
a tempo
naturale
377

382
Gtr. 1
Gtr. 2
386
Gtr. 1
Gtr. 2
389
Gtr. 1
Gtr. 2
f legato
392
Gtr. 1
Gtr. 2
396
Gtr. 1
Gtr. 2

400
Gtr. 1
Gtr. 2
403
Gtr. 1
Gtr. 2
mp
D.C. al Fine Ossia
406
Gtr. 1
ff
Gtr. 2
ff